THE JOY OF
PIANO

It was Signor Bartolommeo Cristofori,
the imaginative instrument maker of Florence, who
in 1709 made the first piano. He probably never envisioned
that his invention the 'piano e forte' would for centuries
be the most popular and widely used of all musical
instruments. And, this 'wonderous box', as
Oliver Wendell Holmes once called it,
continues to grow in popularity. Today, more people
study piano for sheer pleasure than at any time in history.

The Joy Of Piano was compiled and arranged by Denes Agay.
It contains a colourful and well-balanced storehouse
of easy-to-play melodies. The player will
enjoy familiar themes by the masters,
folk tunes, favourite standard songs and popular
melodies of today. The variety is pleasing and educational.
Mr. Agay's musical arrangements are simple and
full sounding. Pianists of all ages will
appreciate the musical quality that has
made his work so widely known.

Published by
Hal Leonard

Exclusive Distributors:
Hal Leonard
7777 West Bluemound Road, Milwaukee, WI 53213
Email: info@halleonard.com
Hal Leonard Europe Limited
42 Wigmore Street Marylebone, London, WIU 2 RY
Email: info@halleonardeurope.com
Hal Leonard Australia Pty. Ltd.
4 Lentara Court Cheltenham, Victoria, 9132 Australia
Email: info@halleonard.com.au

Order No. YK21103
ISBN: 978-0-7119-0131-5
This book © Copyright 1968, 2014 Yorktown Music Press Inc.

Printed in the EU.
www.halleonard.com

Contents

Symphony No. 7

(Theme from 2nd Movement)

Ludwig van Beethoven

Allegretto

Symphony No.1
(Theme - Finale)

Johannes Brahms

Moderate, steady motion

Lullaby

Johannes Brahms

Slowly, tenderly

Caprice No. 24

Niccolo Paganini

New World Symphony

(Theme from 2nd Movement)

Anton Dvorak

Slowly

Piano Concerto No. 3
(Theme from 1st Movement)

Ludwig van Beethoven

Piano Concerto
(Theme)

Edvard Grieg

Moderately fast

Pomp and Circumstance

Edward Elgar

Broadly and solemnly

Nocturne

Moderately

Frederic Chopin

Tempo indication in the original is $\frac{12}{8}$

Saint Anthony Chorale

Joseph Haydn

Moderate walking tempo

Sheep May Safely Graze

(Theme from the "Birthday Cantata")

Johann Sebastian Bach

Gently moving

Unfinished Symphony
(Theme)

Franz Schubert

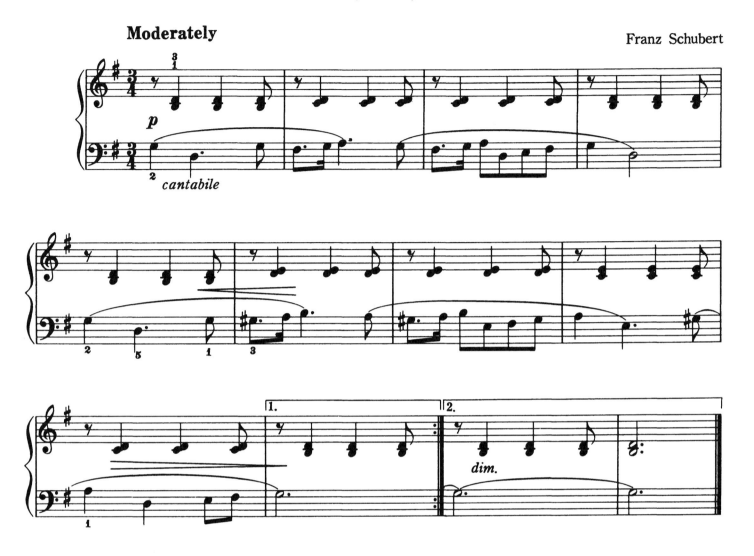

To A Wild Rose

Edward MacDowell

Piano Concerto No. 1

(Theme from 1st Movement)

Peter I. Tchaikovsky

Moderately broad

con ped.

Symphony No.5

(Theme from 2nd Movement)

Peter I. Tchaikovsky

Slowly

Clair de Lune

Slowly, with expression

Claude Debussy

Slavonic Dance No. 10

Anton Dvorak

Freely moving

Polovetzian Dance

Alexander Borodin

Comedians' Galop

Dmitri Kabalevsky

Hungarian Dance No. 4

Johannes Brahms

Gavotte
(from Violin Sonata No. 6)

Graceful walking tempo

Johann Sebastian Bach

Farandole
(from L'Arlesienne Suite No. 2)

Georges Bizet

Mattinata

Freely moving

Ruggiero Leoncavallo

Waltzes by Strauss
(Themes)

Moderately

"The Emperor Waltz"

Johann Strauss

"Vienna Life"

Lively

"Wine, Women, and Song"

La Ci Darem La Mano
(Duet from "Don Giovanni")

Wolfgang A. Mozart

Comfortable walking tempo

Toreador Song
(from "Carmen")

Georges Bizet

Moderately, with vigor

Madame Butterfly
(Themes)

Giacomo Puccini

Broadly

My Heart At Thy Sweet Voice
(from "Samson and Delilah")

Moderately slow

Camille Saint-Saëns

The Bell Song
(from "Lakmé")

Leo Delibes

Very lively

Tit - Willow
(from "The Mikado")

William S. Gilbert

Arthur Sullivan

Moderately, with warmth

Pirate Chorus
(from "The Pirates Of Penzance")

William S. Gilbert

Arthur Sullivan

Moderate march tempo

The Merry Widow Waltz

Moderate waltz tempo

Franz Lehár

Toyland
(from "Babes In Toyland")

Glen MacDonough

Victor Herbert

Glow Worm

Lila Cayley Robinson

Paul Lincke

Beautiful Dreamer

Stephen Foster

Mighty Lak' A Rose

Ethelbert Nevin

When The Saints Come Marchin' In

Spirited walking tempo

Traditional

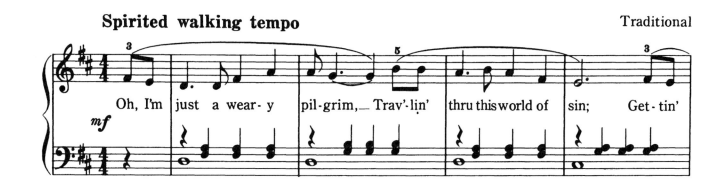

Oh, I'm just a wear-y pil-grim,— Trav'-lin' thru this world of sin; Get-tin'

read-y for the day — When the saints come march-in' in.— Oh, when the

saints— come march-in' in, When the saints come march-in' in, Lord, I

want to be in that num-ber,— When the saints come march-in' in.

Sweet Betsy From Pike

Moderately bright

Folk Song

Did you ev-er hear tell of sweet Bet-sy from Pike, Who cross'd the wide

prai-ries with her lov-er Ike? With two yoke of ox-en, A

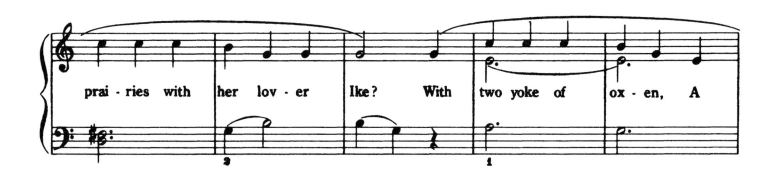

big yal-ler dog, A tall Shang-hai roost-er, And one spot-ted

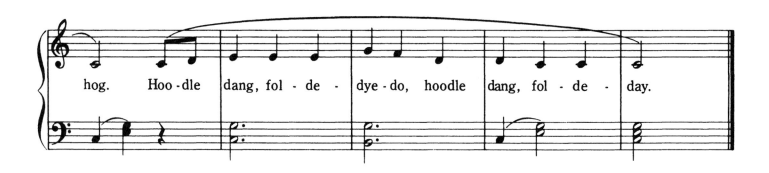

hog. Hoo-dle dang, fol-de-dye-do, hoodle dang, fol-de-day.

When I Was Single

Lively and robust

Folk Song

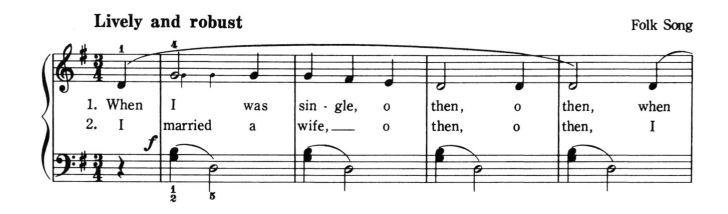

1. When I was sin - gle, o then, o then, when
2. I married a wife, — o then, o then, I

I was sin - gle, o then, — When I was
married a wife, — o then, — I married a

sin - gle my pock - ets did jin - gle, I wish I was sin - gle a -
wife, she's the curse of my life, — I wish I was sin - gle a -

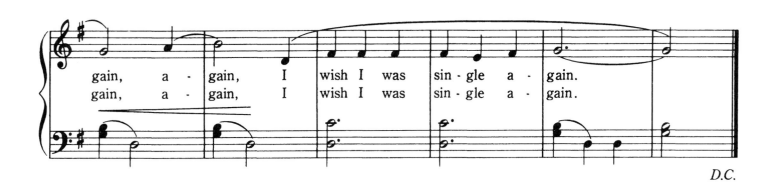

gain, a - gain, I wish I was sin - gle a - gain.
gain, a - gain, I wish I was sin - gle a - gain.

D.C.

Li'l Liza Jane

Folk Song

Bright

I know a gal that I a - dore, Li'l Li - za Jane,

'Way down south in Bal - ti - more, Li'l Li - za Jane.

Oh, E - li - za, Li'l Li - za Jane,

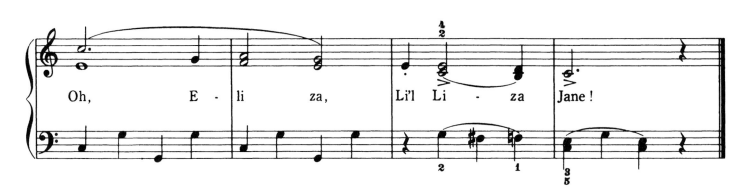

Oh, E - li - za, Li'l Li - za Jane!

Red River Valley

Cowboy Song

Lively

1. From this valley they say you are go-ing,_____ I will
sit by my side if you love me,_____ Do not

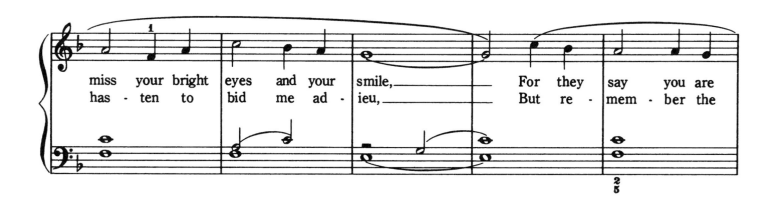

miss your bright eyes and your smile,_____ For they say you are
has-ten to bid me ad-ieu,_____ But re-mem-ber the

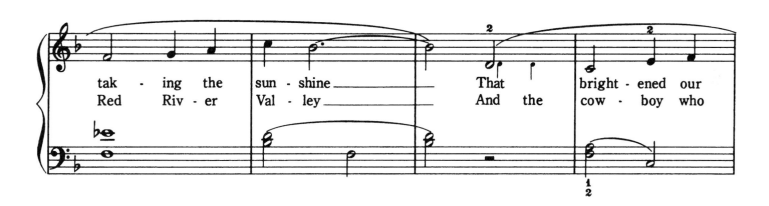

tak-ing the sun-shine_____ That the bright-ened our
Red Riv-er Val-ley_____ And the cow-boy who

path-way a-while._____ 2. Come and
loved you so true.

Polly Wolly Doodle

Traditional

Lively

Oh I went down South for to see my Sal, sing-ing Pol-ly Wol-ly Doo-dle all the

day; Oh my Sal, she is such a spunk-y gal, Sings Pol-ly Wol-ly Doo-dle all the

day. Fare thee well, Fare thee well, Fare thee well my fair-y fay, For I'm

gwine to Lou-si-an-na, my gui-tar and her "pi-an-a," Sing-ing Pol-ly Wol-ly Doo-dle all the day.

The Yellow Rose Of Texas

Bright

Traditional

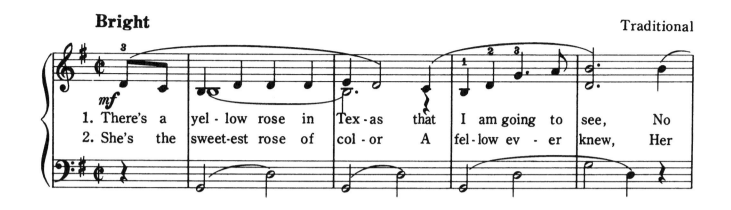

1. There's a yel-low rose in Tex-as that I am going to see, No
2. She's the sweet-est rose of col-or A fel-low ev-er knew, Her

oth-er fel-low knows her, No fel-low on-ly me, She___
eyes are bright as di'-monds, They spark-le like the dew, You may

cried so when I left her, It like to break my heart, And
talk a-bout your dear-est May, And sing of Ro - sa Lee', But the

if I ev-er find her We nev-er more will part.
yel-low rose of Tex-as beats the belles of Ten-nes-see.

D.C.

Down By The Riverside
(I Ain't Gonna Study War No More)

Moderately with spirit

Folk Song

Gon-na lay down my sword and shield, Down by the riv-er-side, Down by the riv-er-side, Down by the riv-er-side, Gon-na lay down my sword and shield, Down by the riv-er-side, I'll stud-y war no more. I ain't gon-na stu-dy war no more, I ain't gon-na stud-y war no more, I ain't gon-na stud-y for war no more.

The Blue Tail Fly

Folk Song

I've Been Workin' On The Railroad

Happy walking tempo

Traditional

Down In The Valley

Moderately

Folk Song

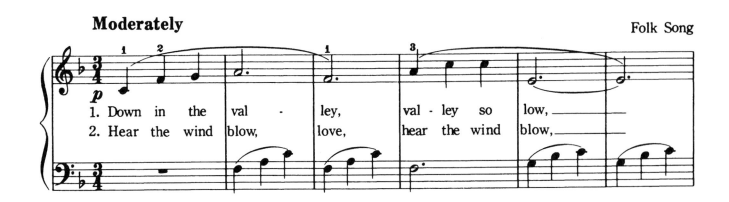

1. Down in the val - ley, val - ley so low,
2. Hear the wind blow, love, hear the wind blow,

Hang your head o - ver, hear the wind blow.
Hang your head o - ver, hear the wind blow.

Aunt Rhody Boogie

Traditional
adapted by Denes Agay

Lively boogie tempo

mf

Fascination

Filippo D. Marchetti

Slow waltz

Amoureuse
(Valse Continentale)

Slow waltz

Rudolphe Berger

Moscow Nights

V. Soloviev- Sedoy

Moderately

The Whistler And His Dog

Moderate walking tempo

Arthur Pryor

D.C. al Fine

The Kerry Dance

James L. Molloy

Loch Lomond

Walking tempo

Scotch Air

Parade Of The Tin Soldiers

Leon Jessel

Lively and gracefully

D.C. al Fine

Down South

Bright, strutting tempo

W. H. Myddleton

Chicken Reel

Lively

Traditional Fiddle Tune

When You Were Sweet Sixteen

James Thornton

Moderately slow

Sweet Adeline

Richard H. Gerard

Harry Armstrong

Moderately slow

Sweet A - del - ine, My A - de - line,

At night, dear heart, For you I pine;

In all my dreams, Your fair face beams,

You're the flow-er of my heart, Sweet A - de - line.

In My Merry Oldsmobile

Vincent Bryant

Gus Edwards

The Band Played On

John F. Palmer

Charles B. Ward

Daisy Bell
(Bicycle Built For Two)

Harry Dacre

Bright waltz tempo

My Gal Sal

Paul Dresser

They called her fri-vo-lous Sal, — A pe-cu - liar sort of a gal, — With a heart that was mel-low, An all 'round good fel-low, Was my old pal. — Your trou-bles, sor-rows and care, — She was al - ways will-ing to share. — A wild sort of dev-il, But dead on the lev-el, Was my gal Sal.

Give My Regards To Broadway

George M. Cohan

Brightly

Wait 'Till The Sun Shines, Nellie

Andrew B. Sterling

Harry von Tilzer

I Love You Truly

Rather slow

Carrie Jacobs-Bond

1. I love you tru - ly, tru - ly dear,
2. Ah! love, 'tis some - thing to feel your kind hand,

Life with its sor - row, life with its tear,
Ah! yes, 'tis some - thing by your with side to stand;

Fades in - to dreams when I feel you are near,
Gone is the sor - row, gone doubt and fear,

rit.

For I love you tru - ly, tru - ly, dear.

Dear Old Girl

Richard Henry Buck

Theodore F. Morse

Rather slow

mp Dear Old Girl, the rob-in sings a-bove you, Dear Old Girl, it speaks of how I love you; The blind-ing tears are fall-ing, As I think of my lost pearl, And my brok-en heart is call-ing, Call-ing for you, Dear Old Girl.

Hello! Ma Baby

Howard and Emerson

When Johnny Comes Marching Home

Lively march tempo

Traditional

America, The Beautiful

Katherine L. Bates

Samuel A. Ward

Moderately

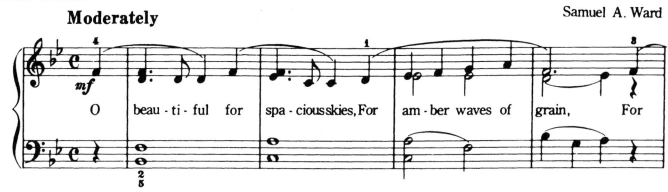

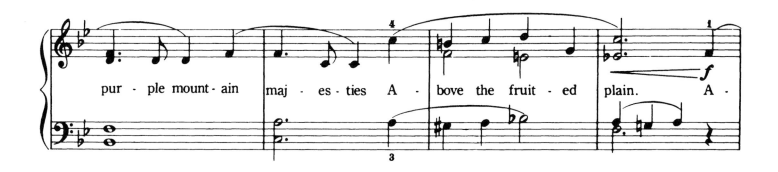

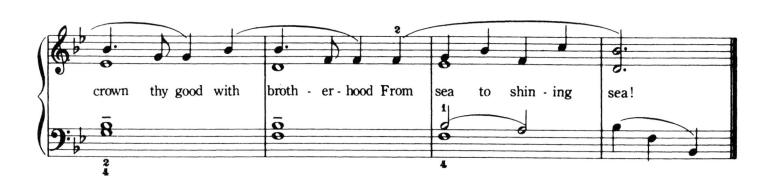